Personal Finance Book

Alejandro Rivera

/ Alejandro Rivera /

Legal and legal data
Author: © Alejandro Rivera
All rights reserved

The Work is protected by copyright laws and international treaties. The Author owns all copyrights in the Work, including, but not limited to, the rights of reproduction, distribution, display and adaptation. Any unauthorized use of the Work, including but not limited to reproduction, distribution or public display, is strictly prohibited and may constitute a violation of the Author's copyright.

Copyright holder: © Imperial Edition

/ Alejandro Rivera /

Personal Budget

The personal budget is a crucial tool to optimally manage individual finances. It involves detailed planning of income and expenses over a specific period, usually monthly. Income must be identified, including salaries, fees and any additional income, with consideration of taxes and deductions to calculate actual net income.

Regarding expenses, basic needs should be prioritized, such as housing, food, transportation and public services. Additionally, a percentage is allocated for discretionary spending, such as entertainment, dining, and shopping. It is crucial to allocate part of your income to savings and manage debt payments, such as loans and credit cards.

Creating a budget involves a detailed record of each income and expense, as well as defining short- and long-term financial goals, such as savings or future investments. Adjusting the budget according to needs and changes in income or expenses is essential to maintain its realism and achieve financial goals.

Constant monitoring of the budget is key. A periodic review should be conducted to evaluate progress toward financial goals and make adjustments as necessary. Practical tips include prioritizing needs over wants, establishing an emergency fund, avoiding unnecessary debt, and using tools and apps for tracking and control. In short, a well-structured personal budget is essential for maintaining a healthy financial balance and working toward specific financial goals.

The personal budget is an essential tool in individual financial management, offering an organized and planned view of income and expenses. In its creation, it is essential to identify all sources of income, which go beyond salaries, including additional income such as bonuses, royalties or any other financial income. Calculating net income, after taxes and deductions, provides an accurate basis for financial planning.

Expenses, on the other hand, must be carefully categorized. Basic needs, such as housing, food and utilities, must be prioritized. Allocating resources for discretionary spending, such as entertainment and leisure, is done with the goal of balancing financial life. Likewise, dedicating a portion of your income to savings is crucial to creating a financial cushion and preparing for emergencies.

Creating specific financial goals is another essential component of your personal budget. Setting short- and long-term goals, whether for purchasing a home, educating children, or retirement, provides a clear framework for allocating resources. Additionally, budget flexibility allows for adjustments as circumstances change, such as changes in income, unforeseen expenses, or new financial goals.

Constant monitoring of the budget is key to its effectiveness. Periodically reviewing results allows you to evaluate progress toward financial goals and make adjustments as necessary. Additionally, continued financial education is essential to improve understanding of money management and making informed decisions.

In short, personal budgeting is not only a practical tool for efficient resource allocation, but also a means to cultivate financial responsibility and work toward meaningful financial goals.

Savings and Investment

Saving and investing are two fundamental aspects of personal financial management, each with its own objectives and strategies. Saving is the process of setting aside a portion of income for future use, whether to meet emergencies, achieve short-term goals, or build a retirement fund. This practice provides financial security and flexibility, allowing you to face unforeseen expenses without resorting to debt and facilitating the achievement of planned objectives.

Investing, on the other hand, involves putting money to work to generate returns over time. Unlike saving, which is generally held in savings accounts with low returns, investing seeks higher returns through participation in financial instruments such as stocks, bonds, real estate or mutual funds. The primary goal of investing is to grow capital over time and beat inflation to preserve and increase purchasing power.

It is essential to recognize that both saving and investing play complementary roles in a sound financial strategy. Saving provides stability and immediate liquidity, while investing offers the opportunity to generate higher returns, although with an associated level of risk. Diversification, or spreading resources across different asset classes, is a common strategy for balancing risk and return in the investment space.

Successful financial planning involves how much will determine where savings and investments go, based on goals and time horizon. A balanced approach that combines saving for immediate needs with investing for long-term goals helps build a solid financial foundation. Additionally, continued financial education is essential to understanding the various investment vehicles available and making informed decisions that align with personal financial goals. In summary, better integrating saving and investing into personal financial planning is key to achieving financial stability and long-term growth.

Saving and investing represent two fundamental pillars in financial management, each playing specific roles in building financial health and achieving long-term goals. Saving, at its most basic essence, involves setting aside a portion of income for future use. This act of financial precaution provides a safety net against unforeseen events and helps maintain economic stability. In addition, saving allows you to meet short-term goals, such as purchasing goods or taking trips, without incurring significant debt.

On the other hand, investment enters the world of generating returns through the deployment of funds in different financial vehicles. Investments go beyond the simple accumulation of money and seek to increase capital over time. Stocks, bonds, real estate, and mutual funds are just a few of the options available to those seeking more substantial returns than those offered by traditional savings accounts. Investing, however, carries a certain degree of risk, as financial markets can be volatile.

In comprehensive financial planning, finding the right balance between saving and investing is essential. Savings provide a solid foundation, ensuring the availability of liquid resources for emergencies and short-term needs. On the other hand, investment allows you to grow your assets and combat the erosive effects of inflation over time. Diversifying investments, distributing funds across different asset classes, is a key strategy to mitigate risks.

In conclusion, savings and investment, although different in their approach, collaborate harmoniously in building a robust financial future. The smart combination of saving for immediate stability and investing for long-term growth is a sound strategy. Understanding personal financial goals, risk tolerance, and continuing education are critical factors in making informed decisions and achieving financial success throughout life.

Debt Reduction

Debt reduction is an essential component in responsible financial management and the path to long-term economic stability. This process involves the progressive decrease of the amount owed, whether in the form of loans, credit cards or other financial obligations. Addressing debt systematically not only alleviates the current financial burden, but also helps free up resources for other priorities, such as saving and investing.

The first step in debt reduction is to understand and list all existing financial obligations. This includes student loans, mortgages, credit card balances, and any other outstanding debt. Once identified, the interest rates associated with each debt can be evaluated, allowing those with higher rates to be prioritized, thus maximizing the impact of reduction efforts.

Developing a structured payment plan is key to the debt reduction process. This plan could follow different strategies, such as the "snowball" method (tackle smaller debts first) or the "higher interest rate first" approach (tackle debts with higher interest rates) . Consolidating debt or renegotiating interest rates with lenders may also be an option, depending on financial situation and feasibility.

In addition, it is essential to establish a solid budget that allows specific funds to be allocated for debt reduction. Redefining priorities and making lifestyle adjustments to channel more resources toward paying off debt contributes significantly to the success of this process. Maintaining financial discipline and avoiding the accumulation of new debt are essential practices to ensure constant progress in reducing financial burden.

Not only does debt reduction have short-term benefits, such as improving liquidity and reducing financial stress, but it also lays the foundation for long-term financial health. As debt decreases, resources are freed up for other financial goals, such as saving for retirement, education, or investing. Additionally, improved credit history can have positive effects on your ability to obtain favorable interest rates in the future.

Reducing debt is a key financial process to free yourself from significant financial burdens and move towards lasting financial stability. This goal involves careful evaluation of financial obligations, including loans, credit cards and other outstanding debts. Understanding the nature of each debt and its terms, as well as identifying spending patterns that contribute to debt accumulation, are essential steps in the reduction process.

A central aspect of debt reduction is negotiating with lenders to improve loan terms. This could include the possibility of consolidating debt to simplify payments or seeking agreements to reduce interest rates. Many lenders are willing to work with debtors to facilitate the payment process and avoid late payments.

In addition, creating a detailed budget becomes a fundamental tool in managing finances during debt reduction. Setting clear goals, allocating specific portions of income toward debt repayment, and continually monitoring progress are effective practices. Financial discipline, such as avoiding unnecessary expenses and maintaining a lean lifestyle, becomes crucial to freeing up additional resources for debt repayment.

Exploring additional sources of income can speed up the debt reduction process. Considering supplemental income opportunities, such as part-time jobs, freelancing, or sales of unwanted items, can generate additional funds to address financial obligations more efficiently.

It is important to note that debt reduction not only involves eliminating outstanding balances, but also adopting healthy long-term financial habits. Developing a responsible spending mindset and learning to live within the limits of disposable income are valuable lessons that last long after you've paid off debt.

In short, debt reduction goes beyond simply paying what you owe. It requires a thorough assessment of personal finances, active negotiation with lenders, adoption of conscious spending habits, and dedication to a structured repayment plan. By achieving this balance, individuals can not only free themselves from financial burden, but also lay the foundation for a stronger, debt-free financial future.

Retirement Planning

Retirement planning is a crucial process that involves financial preparation and strategic decision making to ensure a comfortable and secure retirement. One of the first steps in this process is to evaluate personal retirement goals. This involves considering your desired lifestyle, potential medical expenses, and any other long-term goals. By having a clear vision of your goals, you can establish a solid and realistic financial plan.

Identifying and estimating retirement income is another key aspect of planning. This includes evaluating sources of income, such as social security, pensions, personal savings, and potential investment income. Calculating how much is needed to maintain the desired standard of living during retirement allows us to determine the sufficiency of the resources accumulated up to that point.

Creating a specific retirement budget is essential. This budget should consider both essential and discretionary expenses, considering possible increases in health care costs and other age-related needs. Planning ahead for health expenses is particularly critical, as medical costs tend to increase in retirement.

Diversifying retirement assets is a vital strategy to mitigate risks and maximize returns. Investing in a mix of stocks, bonds and other financial instruments can help balance risk and return over time. Additionally, adjusting asset allocation as you approach retirement to reduce risk exposure is also common practice.

Establishing a specific emergency fund for retirement is an additional precaution that can provide financial security. This fund should cover unforeseen expenses, such as home repairs, unexpected medical expenses, or any other financial setbacks that may arise during retirement.

Retirement planning is a dynamic process that requires periodic review and adjustment. Changes in personal, financial and health circumstances can influence the effectiveness of the original plan, so flexibility and adaptability are essential. Additionally, continued education on financial topics and updates to retirement laws and policies are essential to making informed decisions.

Retirement planning is a process that goes beyond purely financial considerations, also addressing emotional and lifestyle aspects. First of all, it is essential to visualize the type of life you want to lead during retirement. This includes choosing a possible place of residence, free time activities and any project or trip you wish to undertake. Retirement not only means the cessation of work, but also the opportunity to explore new passions and enjoy a fuller life.

Health plays a crucial role in retirement planning. Considering healthcare, both in terms of coverage and potential costs, is essential. Choosing an appropriate health plan and estimating future medical expenses are key to ensuring a peaceful and healthy retirement. In addition, adopting healthy lifestyle habits before retirement can have a significant impact on the quality of life later.

Succession planning is another important component. Ensuring legal documents, such as wills and powers of attorney, are in order is essential to protecting assets and facilitating the transition of wealth to future generations. This also includes considerations around asset distribution and tax minimization, ensuring a smooth and effective transition.

Participation in educational and personal development activities during retirement is a growing trend. Many people choose to continue learning and contributing to the community through volunteering, mentoring, or participating in courses and workshops. This approach not only enriches personal life, but can also have positive benefits for mental and emotional health during retirement.

Retirement planning should also address free time management in a meaningful way. Maintaining structure and establishing daily routines contributes to a smoother transition to retirement.

Additionally, exploring hobbies, social engagement, and participating in recreational activities can fill free time with enriching and satisfying experiences.

In short, retirement planning is a multidimensional process that encompasses financial, health, inheritance and lifestyle aspects. By considering all of these elements, individuals can create a complete and holistic retirement plan that not only ensures financial stability, but also a retirement filled with purpose, health, and personal satisfaction.

Personal Insurance

Personal insurance plays an essential role in financial management and protecting individual well-being. One of the most fundamental types of insurance is life insurance, designed to provide financial support to beneficiaries in the event of the death of the insured. This type of insurance can help cover expenses such as loans, mortgages, or educational expenses, ensuring that loved ones do not face financial hardship during an emotionally difficult time.

Another important aspect of personal insurance is health insurance. This type of policy provides coverage for medical expenses, including doctor visits, hospitalization, medications, and medical procedures. With healthcare costs rising, health insurance has become crucial to protecting individuals' financial assets and ensuring access to quality medical services.

Disability insurance is another form of personal protection that deserves attention. In the event that an injury or illness prevents a person from working, disability insurance provides income replacement to help cover living and medical expenses. This form of insurance offers an important financial safety net, especially when earned income is a vital component of livelihood.

Car insurance is mandatory in many places and provides coverage in case of accidents or damage to the vehicle. In addition to meeting legal requirements, auto insurance offers financial protection in unforeseen situations, covering the costs of vehicle repair or replacement, as well as medical expenses associated with traffic accidents.

Estate planning also includes personal insurance, such as home insurance. This type of policy protects the home and its contents against loss and damage caused by events such as fire, flood or theft. Additionally, it may include civil liability, covering injuries or damages to third parties within the property.

The choice of personal insurance should be based on careful evaluation of individual and family needs. Insurance professionals can provide personalized advice to determine the appropriate level of coverage and select policies that best fit your particular circumstances. In addition, periodic review of policies is essential to ensure that coverage adjusts to life changes, such as marriages, births or property acquisition.

The variety of personal insurance available covers various areas of daily life and offers protection against unforeseen situations. One of the most relevant insurances is civil liability insurance, which covers damages caused to third parties in the event of accidents or injuries in which the insured is considered responsible. This type of insurance is essential to protect personal assets and avoid devastating financial consequences in cases of lawsuits.

Travel insurance is another important category that provides coverage while traveling. Includes compensation for cancellations, trip interruptions, lost luggage and medical expenses abroad. This form of insurance provides travelers with peace of mind and serves as a financial safeguard against unforeseen events that may arise during the trip.

Income insurance, also known as disability or sick income insurance, offers protection in situations where a person is unable to work due to illness or injury. Provides benefits that replace income lost during the period of disability, ensuring financial stability even when earning capacity is impaired.

For those with significant debt, debt settlement insurance or payment protection insurance can be a valuable option. This type of policy covers payments on loans, credit cards or other obligations in the event of job loss, disability or death. It provides a financial safety net to avoid the burden of outstanding debts in difficult circumstances.

Long-term care insurance is another relevant component, especially for financial planning in retirement. This type of insurance covers costs associated with long-term care at home, in a long-term care facility, or through health care services in the event of a chronic illness or disability. Helps preserve savings and assets for financial well-being during retirement.

In the digital age, cyber insurance has emerged as an essential protection. Provides coverage against data loss, identity theft, and other cybersecurity-related risks. As technology plays an increasingly significant role in everyday life, cyber insurance becomes a vital tool for protecting personal and financial information.

In conclusion, personal insurance is not only limited to protecting against physical risks, but covers a wide range of situations and contingencies. Personal insurance selection should be tailored to individual circumstances and financial objectives, providing a safety net in everyday life and against unforeseen events.

Estate Planning

Estate planning is a strategic process that seeks to manage and distribute a person's assets and resources effectively, ensuring the proper preservation and transmission of wealth over time. This process involves a thorough evaluation of assets, liabilities, income, and financial objectives, with the goal of designing a comprehensive plan that reflects the individual's intentions regarding his or her assets.

A central component of estate planning is the creation of a will. This legal document is essential to clearly express how assets should be distributed after death. Additionally, it appoints guardians for minors, establishes trusts, and may include instructions regarding medical and disability care issues. The will is a vital tool to ensure that the individual's wishes are fulfilled and that the transition of wealth is smooth.

Trusts also play a prominent role in estate planning. These legal instruments allow the individual to transfer assets to a trustee for management and distribution according to established specifications. Trusts can offer benefits such as tax reduction, asset protection, and controlled allocation of resources over time, providing flexibility and security to estate planning.

Estate planning is not limited to the distribution of assets after death; It also addresses strategies to minimize tax obligations. Tax anticipation and mitigation are critical aspects of this process, and may include the utilization of tax exemptions, charitable giving, and the implementation of efficient tax structures, such as irrevocable trusts.

Life insurance becomes a key tool in estate planning. In addition to providing benefits for beneficiaries after death, life insurance can help cover estate taxes and provide liquidity to cover final expenses and debts. The right choice of life insurance policy and its effective integration into your estate planning strategy can make a significant difference in wealth preservation.

The estate planning process should be reviewed and adjusted over time to reflect changes in financial and family situations, as well as changes in tax laws and regulations. Life is full of changes, such as marriages, births, divorces or significant changes in financial situation, and estate planning must be flexible enough to adapt to these changing circumstances.

Estate planning is a comprehensive process that goes beyond the mere distribution of assets and seeks to ensure the sustainability, growth and protection of wealth throughout generations. In this context, asset diversification emerges as a fundamental principle. The strategic allocation of investments in various asset classes, such as bonds, real estate and other financial vehicles, not only seeks to optimize returns, but also mitigate the risks associated with market volatility, thus ensuring the stability of family wealth.

Financial education and preparing future generations for wealth management are essential elements in estate planning. This involves imparting financial knowledge, instilling values related to fiscal responsibility and fostering a sound understanding of financial management. The creation of educational structures and the active participation of heirs in financial decision-making contribute to preserving and strengthening assets over time.

Estate planning also addresses issues related to protection against potential legal and financial contingencies. Creating legal structures, such as family partnerships, trusts, and prenuptial agreements, can provide protection against family disputes, divorces, and other unforeseen events. These measures not only protect assets legally, but also establish clear protocols for decision-making and asset management.

Social and philanthropic impact have become a growing consideration in estate planning. Many people choose to integrate philanthropic strategies into their estate plans, establishing foundations, charitable giving, or charitable trusts. These initiatives not only allow you to contribute to meaningful causes, but they can also generate tax benefits and pass on family values across generations.

Additionally, estate planning can include strategies for succession in family businesses. This process involves the successful transition of leadership and ownership of the company to future generations. Identifying and preparing successors, implementing corporate governance structures, and considering exit strategies are key aspects of ensuring the continuity and prosperity of the family business.

In short, estate planning goes beyond simple asset distribution and addresses crucial aspects such as investment diversification, financial education, legal protection, social impact and succession in family businesses. By taking a holistic approach, estate planning strategies can provide stability and sustainability across generations, building a lasting legacy that transcends the financial realm.

/ Alejandro Rivera /

Additional sources of income

Finding additional sources of income is a key strategy in personal financial management that can provide financial stability and improve quality of life. One of the most common options is generating additional income through side jobs or part-time jobs. This approach not only brings additional income, but also diversifies sources of earnings, reducing dependence on a single employer and strengthening financial security. Additionally, part-time work can accommodate diverse talents and skills, allowing people to capitalize on their strengths and explore new areas of interest.

Investment is another significant avenue to generate additional income. Placing money in financial instruments, such as stocks, bonds, real estate or mutual funds, can generate returns and contribute to capital growth. Investment diversification is crucial to mitigate risks and optimize results over time. Investing not only offers the possibility of passive income, but also facilitates wealth accumulation and building long-term wealth.

Entrepreneurship and creating your own business represent an attractive option for those looking for additional sources of income. Whether through creating an online company, providing freelance services, or launching a brick-and-mortar business, entrepreneurship provides the opportunity to capitalize on individual skills and meet market needs. Although it involves greater risk, it also offers significant potential for financial rewards and the freedom to control one's career path.

The gig economy has emerged as a flexible source of additional income for many people. Freelancing jobs, such as driving ride-hailing services, performing tasks through freelancing platforms, or providing online consulting services, allow people to leverage their skills and generate income autonomously. This way of working offers flexibility in terms of hours and location, which can be especially attractive to those looking to balance multiple responsibilities.

Developing additional skills can also become a source of income. Training and certification in specific areas can open opportunities for consulting, mentoring or teaching, generating income through the transmission of knowledge. Online platforms offer numerous opportunities to teach or consult in various fields, turning knowledge and experience into a valuable source of income.

The search for additional sources of income is a fundamental component in contemporary financial management, especially in a dynamic and changing economic environment. An increasingly relevant strategy is participation in the digital economy through online income generation platforms. From creating and selling artisanal products on online marketplaces to participating in affiliate programs or creating content on social media platforms, the digital economy offers various opportunities to monetize skills and passions. This trend reflects the growing importance of online presence and the ability to capitalize on global connectivity to generate additional revenue.

Intellectual property has also become a significant source of income for many creative individuals. Creating and selling digital content, such as e-books, music, photographs, or online courses, allows creators to monetize their talent directly. Specialized platforms facilitate the distribution and commercialization of these intangible assets, opening new avenues for generating income without depending on traditional publishing or distribution structures.

Participating in rewards and loyalty programs has become a popular strategy for accumulating additional income and benefits. Many companies offer programs that reward customer loyalty with points, discounts, or even cash. These programs can range from rewards credit cards to apps that offer discounts on purchases, providing opportunities to earn additional benefits simply by making everyday transactions.

The sharing economy has transformed the way people access goods and services, while providing opportunities to generate additional income.

Property rental platforms, shared transportation services or participation in specific tasks and projects through specific applications offer people the possibility of using their resources efficiently and generating income without the need for full-time employment.

Finally, investing in cryptocurrencies and emerging technologies has emerged as an attractive alternative for those interested in exploring innovative financial opportunities. Acquiring and managing cryptoassets, as well as participating in blockchain technology projects, can offer significant returns, albeit with a higher level of risk. This form of investment represents a change in the traditional conception of financial assets and highlights the importance of being aware of emerging financial trends.

In summary, diversifying income sources goes beyond conventional strategies and involves adapting to the opportunities offered by the digital economy, intellectual property, rewards programs, the collaborative economy and new forms of investment. By embracing these trends and exploring various sources of income, individuals can not only improve their financial stability but also participate in an ever-evolving economic landscape.

Tax Planning

Tax planning is an essential discipline in financial management that seeks to optimize the tax burden in a legal and ethical manner. This process involves anticipating and structuring financial decisions to minimize the taxes paid by an individual or entity. Tax planning is not limited to simply filing tax returns, but encompasses long-term strategies to maximize tax benefits and ensure efficient financial management.

A key aspect of tax planning is evaluating the available tax structures and choosing the most appropriate one based on individual circumstances. This may include decisions about the legal form of ownership, selection of investment account types, income structuring, and estate planning. The right choice of these structures can have a significant impact on the total tax burden over time.

Managing income and deductions is another essential component in tax planning. This involves making informed decisions about the timing of significant income, such as bonuses or asset sales, to minimize tax liabilities. At the same time, identifying and taking advantage of legitimate tax deductions can reduce taxable income, thus contributing to the optimization of the tax bill.

Investment diversification also plays an important role in tax planning. Allocating assets across various investment categories can provide tax benefits by taking advantage of favorable tax treatments. Strategies such as tax loss, where investment losses can offset gains, are common tools in investment tax planning.

Tax planning is deeply influenced by current tax regulations. Therefore, being aware of changes in tax laws and understanding their impact on personal or business finances is crucial. Adaptability to changes in tax policies allows tax planning strategies to be adjusted to maximize benefits and mitigate risks in a dynamic tax environment.

Tax planning also encompasses asset and inheritance management to minimize estate taxes and facilitate the transition of wealth to future generations efficiently. Using legal instruments such as trusts, gifts, and succession structures can help preserve family wealth and reduce the tax consequences associated with the transfer of assets.

Tax planning, from a business perspective, encompasses specific strategies aimed at optimizing an organization's tax burden. A common tactic in this area is international tax planning, which involves managing tax obligations across multiple jurisdictions. Multinational companies, for example, may seek to strategically locate their operations and structures to benefit from favorable tax regimes and reduce exposure to high tax rates. This strategy may include selecting locations for offices or manufacturing centers, managing transfer pricing, and utilizing bilateral tax agreements to optimize the company's overall tax efficiency.

Tax credit management is another essential component in corporate tax planning. Companies can identify and take advantage of available tax credits, which may include incentives for research and development, renewable energy, or hiring employees in certain geographic areas. Optimizing these tax credits not only helps reduce the tax bill, but can also encourage investment in specific areas of the company that generate both economic and fiscal benefits.

Structuring business operations is also a key strategy in tax planning. Choosing the legal form of a business, whether as a corporation, limited liability company or pass-through entity, can have significant implications in terms of tax obligations and legal liability. Careful planning of the business structure can allow companies to take advantage of the tax and operational advantages of each legal form, thus contributing to the efficiency and competitiveness of the business.

Additionally, tax loss management is an important tactic in corporate tax planning. Companies can use net losses from one year to offset profits in subsequent years, thereby reducing the tax burden over time. This strategy allows companies to smooth out fluctuations in their income and expenses, contributing to financial stability throughout economic cycles.

In conclusion, corporate tax planning addresses specific considerations that go beyond personal strategies. International operations management, tax credit optimization, business structuring and tax loss management are key elements that can make a difference in the tax efficiency and competitiveness of a company. Collaborating with specialized tax professionals and constantly monitoring changes in tax laws are essential practices to ensure effective corporate tax planning in compliance with current regulations.

/ Alejandro Rivera /

Financial Emergencies

Financial emergency management is a crucial skill to save individual and family economic stability. Facing unexpected events, such as job loss, unexpected medical expenses, or major repairs, can cause financial stress without proper planning. An essential part of emergency preparedness is creating an emergency fund. This fund, which must be equivalent to several months of expenses, acts as a financial buffer, providing immediate liquidity in crisis situations and avoiding excessive debt.

Diversification of risks is also key in managing financial emergencies. Relying on a single source of income or a specific type of investment can increase vulnerability to unforeseen situations.

Diversifying income sources and maintaining a balanced investment portfolio helps reduce the impact of financial emergencies, allowing for greater flexibility and resilience.

The importance of insurance in emergency management cannot be underestimated. Having adequate insurance policies, such as health insurance, automobile insurance, property insurance, and life insurance, can provide financial protection at critical times. These policies act as a shield against unexpected expenses, ensuring that costs associated with unforeseen events do not fall entirely on personal assets.

Budget planning is another essential tool in managing financial emergencies. Maintaining a detailed and realistic budget allows people to have a clear picture of their income and expenses, identifying areas where adjustments can be made in the event of an emergency. Periodic review of the budget and identification of possible savings areas are practices that strengthen the ability to respond to unforeseen financial situations.

In financial emergency situations, communication and negotiation with creditors and service providers can be essential. Many financial institutions offer financial hardship assistance programs, such as periods of deferment of payments or renegotiation of terms. Maintaining open communication about your financial situation can facilitate temporary arrangements that relieve pressure while you work on long-term solutions.

Financial emergency management becomes a crucial component when facing drastic economic changes or unexpected events. The ability to quickly adapt to unforeseen circumstances is essential to maintaining financial stability. A strategic approach involves identifying and prioritizing essential expenses. By distinguishing between needs and wants, you can establish a plan to reduce non-essential expenses and preserve resources to deal with emergency situations.

Setting realistic financial goals also plays an important role in emergency management. Defining short- and long-term financial goals, such as building an emergency fund or reducing debt, provides a framework for financial decision-making. These goals act as guides during difficult periods, keeping the focus on long-term financial stability.

Income diversification is presented as an effective strategy in emergency management. Creating multiple streams of income, whether through investments, freelancing, or side hustles, can provide an additional financial cushion in times of uncertainty. Adaptability and the search for additional opportunities to generate income contribute to strengthening financial resilience in the face of unforeseen events.

Periodically reviewing and updating your personal financial situation is an important practice. Keeping accurate records of income, expenses, investments, and debt makes it easier to evaluate financial health. This financial transparency allows for the early identification of warning signs and the taking of preventive measures before emergency situations worsen.

Negotiating with financial institutions and creditors is another useful emergency management tactic. Faced with economic difficulties, many entities are willing to collaborate in debt restructuring or extending payment terms. Open communication about financial circumstances allows you to explore options and agreements that will temporarily ease the financial burden.

Continuing financial education also plays a vital role in emergency management. Understanding concepts such as interest rates, investments, and savings strategies provides valuable tools for making informed decisions during challenging economic times. Financial literacy not only contributes to prudent decision-making, but also improves confidence and the ability to address complex financial situations.

In summary, financial emergency management involves a combination of strategic planning, income diversification, constant review of financial situation, and educational skills. The ability to adapt, set clear goals, and maintain a proactive mindset are essential elements to overcoming unexpected financial obstacles and preserving long-term economic stability.

/ Alejandro Rivera /

Influence of technology on personal finances

The influence of technology on personal finances has been profound and transformative, affecting the way we manage, access and make decisions about our financial resources. One of the main contributions of technology is the automation of financial processes. Online applications and platforms allow for the automation of payments, savings and budgets. This simplifies daily tasks, reduces the chance of errors and provides a clear view of spending patterns, making it easier to make informed decisions.

Accessibility to financial information has expanded significantly thanks to technology. Mobile banking apps provide users with instant access to their accounts from anywhere, allowing them to make transactions, check balances, and monitor expenses in real time. This improved accessibility not only streamlines financial operations, but also empowers people by giving them greater control and understanding of their personal finances.

Technology has also revolutionized personal investing. Online investment platforms offer individuals access to a wide range of financial instruments, from stocks and bonds to mutual funds and cryptocurrencies. Artificial intelligence and advanced algorithms make it easy to personalize investment portfolios and offer recommendations based on real-time data analysis. This allows investors to make more informed decisions and adapt investment strategies dynamically.

Financial education has also undergone a significant change thanks to technology. Online platforms offer courses, webinars, and interactive resources that address topics from budget planning to advanced investment strategies. Accessibility to these resources contributes to improving people's financial literacy, enabling them to make more informed and effective decisions regarding their personal finances.

The emergence of digital payment technologies has transformed the way we handle money on a daily basis. The adoption of e-wallets, contactless cards and mobile app payments has reduced dependence on cash and streamlined transactions. This shift towards digital payment methods is not only convenient, but also contributes to financial security by reducing the risks associated with handling cash.

However, the influence of technology on personal finances also presents challenges and ethical considerations. Data security becomes a relevant concern as personal financial information is stored and transmitted across online platforms. Cybersecurity becomes essential to protect users' assets and privacy, highlighting the importance of security awareness and practices in the digital environment.

The influence of technology on personal finances also extends to the emergence of fintech, technology companies specialized in financial services. These innovative companies have introduced disruptive solutions that challenged traditional banking models. Peer-to-peer lending platforms, automated financial advice (robo-advisors) and algorithm-based wealth management services are examples of how fintechs have diversified and democratized access to financial services, providing more flexible and efficient options for consumers. consumers.

Blockchain technology and cryptocurrencies have emerged as key elements in the transformation of the financial landscape. The decentralization and security inherent in blockchain technology have fueled the creation of cryptocurrencies such as Bitcoin and Ethereum, offering alternatives to traditional currencies and raising questions about the future of financial transactions and asset management. Although these technologies are still in a phase of gradual adoption, their potential to disrupt financial paradigms is undeniable.

Artificial intelligence (AI) has significantly improved the personalization of financial services. Chatbots and virtual assistants use AI to interact with users, providing instant responses to queries about accounts, transactions, and spending recommendations. AI-driven automation is also reflected in loan origination and credit decision-making, streamlining processes and offering faster responses to individuals' financial needs.

Augmented reality (AR) and virtual reality (VR) are starting to have an impact on the way people manage their finances. These technologies offer immersive experiences that can make it easier to visualize complex financial data. From virtually exploring real estate properties to visually representing investment portfolios, AR and VR can provide powerful visual tools to improve financial understanding and decision-making.

Despite technological advances, ethics in financial data management and privacy remains a critical concern. Mass data collection by financial and technology companies raises questions about how that data is used and protected. Regulation and the implementation of robust security measures are essential elements to ensure trust and integrity in the field of technology-driven personal finance.

In conclusion, technological evolution has shaped a more dynamic and accessible financial landscape for people. From fintech to blockchain, artificial intelligence and augmented reality, technology continues to offer new possibilities and challenges in managing personal finances. Informed understanding and adaptability are essential to make the most of the opportunities that technology brings in this ever-changing arena.

/ Alejandro Rivera /

Financial inclusion

Financial inclusion is a fundamental concept that focuses on ensuring that all people have access to adequate and financial services to meet their needs. This principle goes beyond simply having a bank account and encompasses the availability of a wide range of financial services, such as credit, insurance, digital payments and investment services. Lack of access to these services can be a significant barrier to economic development and improving the quality of life of marginalized or disadvantaged populations.

One of the key aspects of financial inclusion is overcoming the digital divide. In an increasingly digitalized world, access to technology and connectivity has become crucial to participating in the global economy. Ensuring people have access to mobile devices, internet services, and technology education is essential to integrating those who have historically been excluded from the formal financial system.

Financial institutions play a vital role in promoting financial inclusion. Creating products and services tailored to the needs of unbanked or underserved populations is essential. This can include low-cost accounts, microcredit, huge insurance, and digital payment solutions that adapt to the economic and cultural realities of specific communities. By addressing these specific needs, financial institutions can foster participation and trust in financial services.

Financial technologies, or fintech, have emerged as key enablers of financial inclusion. Mobile payment platforms, peer-to-peer lending apps, and online financial management services have democratized access to financial services, allowing even those without traditional credit history to participate in the economy in a meaningful way. The agility and flexibility of fintech are especially beneficial for reaching populations that are outside the reach of traditional financial institutions.

Financial education also plays a critical role in financial inclusion. Ensuring that people understand the basic principles of money management, saving and investing is essential to empowering them to make informed financial decisions. Educational programs and awareness campaigns can play a key role in this regard, empowering people to use financial services effectively and sustainably.

Financial inclusion not only has individual benefits, but also contributes to sustainable economic development. By giving access to financial services to a greater number of people, business creation, job creation and active participation in the formal economy are encouraged. Furthermore, financial inclusion can contribute to reducing economic inequality by providing equitable opportunities for economic growth and wealth accumulation.

Financial inclusion is a paradigm that focuses on ensuring that all people, regardless of their socioeconomic level or geographic location, have access to financial services that allow them to fully participate in the economy. One of the fundamental pillars of financial inclusion is the creation of solid financial infrastructures, especially in regions where traditional banking services are limited. Establishing bank branches, ATMs, and mobile financial services in rural areas or underserved communities is essential to provide access to services such as deposits, withdrawals, and transfers.

Mainstreaming financial inclusion into government and policy agendas also plays a crucial role. Regulatory frameworks and government initiatives can facilitate the creation of enabling environments for financial inclusion. This may include implementing policies that encourage competition in the financial sector, reducing regulatory barriers for financial institutions, and promoting programs that facilitate access to basic financial services.

Innovation in financial products is also a significant component of financial inclusion. Developing financial solutions tailored to the needs of specific populations, such as microcredit for local entrepreneurs or growth insurance for low-income communities, helps close financial gaps. Collaboration between the private sector, non-governmental organizations and governments can catalyze the development of innovative financial products that address specific challenges in diverse communities.

Technology, particularly mobile telephony, has emerged as an essential catalyst for financial inclusion. Mobile financial services allow people to transact, access banking services and make payments without relying on traditional banking infrastructure. This ability to use technology to circumvent geographic limitations and facilitate access to financial services has been a key factor in the expansion of financial inclusion around the world.

The promotion of financial inclusion is also closely linked to gender equality. Women, in many parts of the world, have faced additional historical barriers to accessing financial services. Initiatives that address these disparities, such as women-specific financial education and microfinance programs aimed at female entrepreneurs, are crucial to ensuring equitable financial inclusion.

In conclusion, financial inclusion does not only imply access to basic services, but encompasses a range of factors ranging from financial infrastructure to product innovation and gender equality. By addressing these aspects comprehensively, an enabling environment is created for all people to actively participate in the economy and improve their economic and social prospects. Financial inclusion, ultimately, stands as an essential pillar to build more equitable and sustainable societies.

/ Alejandro Rivera /

www.ingramcontent.com/pod-product-compliance
Lightning Source LLC
Chambersburg PA
CBHW051816130726
47987CB00003B/1279